UKULELE
SONGS AROUND THE WORLD

by Dick Sheridan

To access audio visit:
www.halleonard.com/mylibrary

"Enter Code"
7207-3233-7492-5021

ISBN 978-1-57424-397-0
SAN 683-8022

Cover by James Creative Group

Cover Ukulele courtesy of Ohana Music, Model #CK-370G

Copyright © 2020 CENTERSTREAM Publishing
P.O. Box 17878 - Anaheim Hills, CA 92817

www.centerstream-usa.com | centerstrm@aol.com | 714-779-9390

More Great Books from Dick Sheridan...

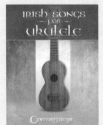

Ukulele Songs Around The World

Ukulele Songs Around The World
By Country

Introduction

They say that music is the universal language. There must be something to this since every corner of the globe is represented by music that is either sung or played on instruments. From simple folk songs to symphonic orchestral arrangements, there's music in the air.

We've taken our ukulele and endeavored to sample some of the world's enormous output of music. Six of the seven continents are represented – North and South America, Africa and Asia, Europe and Australia. There are songs from the English-speaking countries of the United Kingdom – England, Wales and Scotland – along with ballads from Ireland and Australia. Germany, Austria, Poland and other European countries work into the mix, together with songs from Mexico and south of the border. Asia is not forgotten with haunting selections from Japan and China.

We'll waltz Matilda from Australia, jump from France to French Canada, discover beloved songs from Spain and Italy, and range east from Israel to Russia.

And what could be more appropriate for the ukulele than a song from Hawaii? Although originating in Portugal, the instrument was popularized by Hawaiians and is identified with their islands bringing images of swaying palms, rolling surf, and lovely hula dancers strumming their ukes.

It must be said that finding a song from Antarctica presented a problem. It has no countries and no native population. However, many countries have interests in the continent and a number of them are represented in this book. One was inadvertently omitted, and so a song from Argentina was added to represent that frozen southern land – a tango from the country that developed this lively musical form.

Music, like a magic carpet, takes us around the world to savor the familiar and lesser-known. With our ukulele – its melodies and harmonies –we'll scoot to the four corners of the globe and discover just how international that little 4-string instrument can be. You'll see how it captures the drone of the bagpipes, the sound of the balalaika, the lilt of a Norwegian folk dance, the twang of the Japanese samisen and the Chinese moon guitar.

Indeed, we'll be covering a lot of mileage and a lot of music.

Lyrics have mostly been limited to songs in English – like those from the British Isles and Australia. But the melodies of all the other songs speak a universal language and require no transliteration into spoken words.

Are you ready to take that musical journey? Here we go. All aboard! Away we'll go for a musical, magical, memorable grand tour.

ALL THROUGH THE NIGHT

Ukulele tuning: gCEA

Wales

Traditional

Sleep, my child, and peace at-tend thee, all through the night.

Guard - ian an - gels God will send thee, all through the night.

Soft the drow - sy hours are creep - ing, hill and vale in slum - ber steeping.

I my lov - ing vig - il keep - ing all through the night.

ALOHA OE

Hawaii

Ukulele tuning: gCEA

Queen Liliokalani

ALOUETTE

French Canadian

Traditional

Ukulele tuning: gCEA

Sometimes good-naturedly referred to as the national anthem of French Canada, this little song describes plucking different parts of a bird (a lark) -- its beak, its eyes, its ears, and on and on it goes. It's been a time-tested way for children to learn the French names for these bird parts.

The song probably came from France and was popularized during World War I when it was brought back by returning troops to Canada and the United States.

AMERICA THE BEAUTIFUL
America

Katharine Lee Bates Ukulele tuning: gCEA Samuel A. Ward

ASH GROVE

Wales

Ukulele tuning: gCEA

Traditional

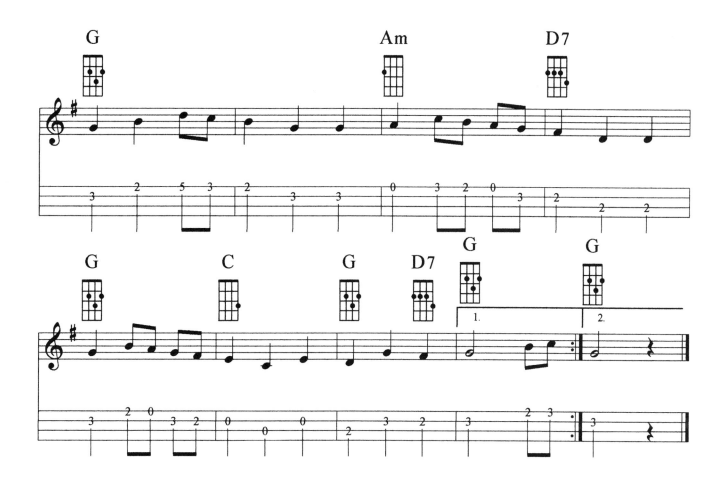

Harlech Castle in Wales

BELIEVE ME
IF ALL THOSE ENDEARING YOUNG CHARMS

Ireland

Ukulele tuning: gCEA

Thomas Moore

BELIEVE ME IF ALL THOSE ENDEAING YOUNG CHARMS

CIELITO LINDO

Mexico

Ukulele tuning: gCEA

Traditional

DARK EYES

Russia

Ukulele tuning: gCEA

Traditional

COME BACK TO SORRENTO
Italy

Ukulele tuning: gCEA

Ernesto De Curtis

DIE GEDANKEN SIND FREI

Germany

Ukulele tuning: gCEA

Traditional

DU, DU LIEGST MIR IM HERZEN

Ukulele tuning: gCEA

German

Traditional

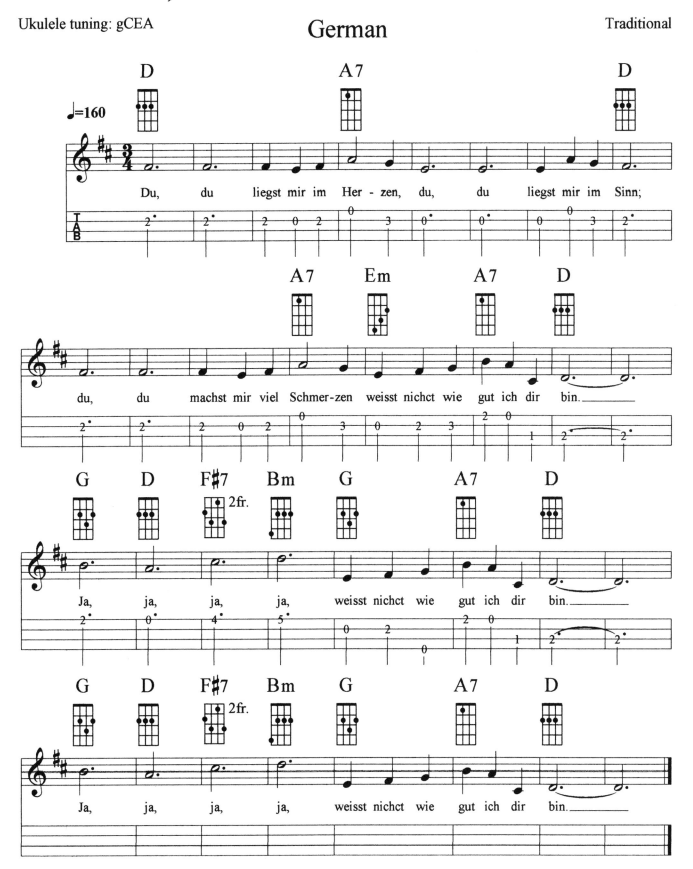

19

EL CHOCLO

Argentina

Ukulele in Low G tuning: GCEA

Angel Villodo

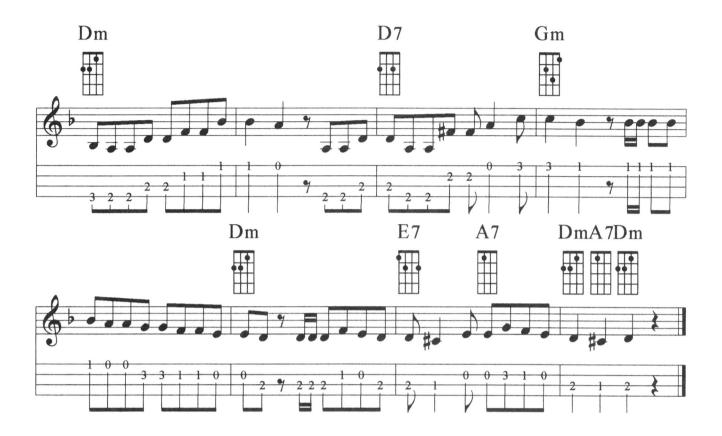

Note: To accomodate the wide range of this song, the tuning of the ukulele was changed to Low G. This tuning drops the 4th string down an octave and the notes are now GCEA.

ELENKE, ELENKE

Bulgaria

Ukulele tuning: gCEA

Traditional

HATIKVA
The National Anthem of Israel

Ukulele tuning: gCEA

Traditional

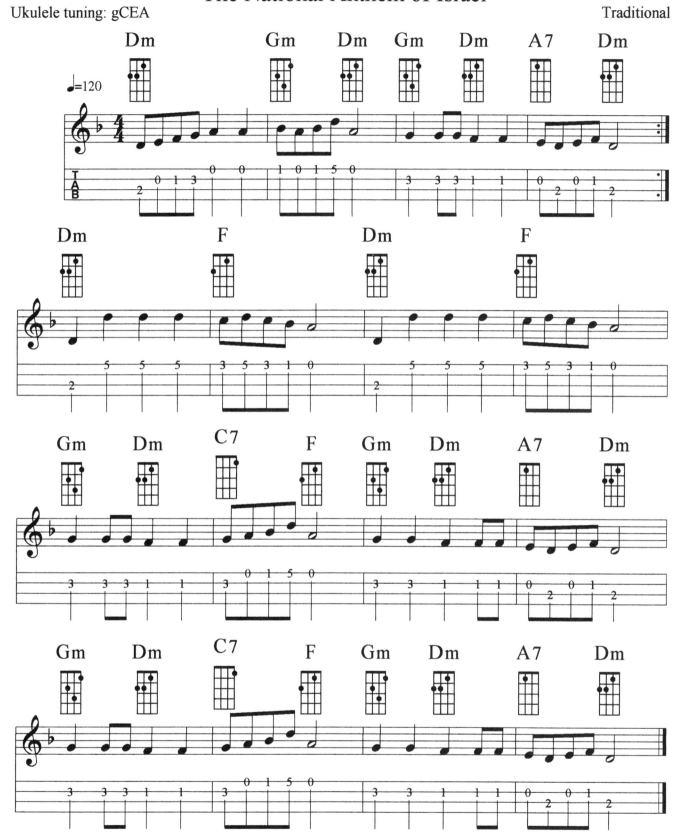

GANGLAT FRAN MOCKFJARD

Sweden

Ukulele in Low G tuning: GCEA

Traditional

GANGLAT FRAN MOCKFJARD

Because of the wide range of this song Low G tuning is used. This lowers the 4th sring to a low G, an octave below the "g" of standard gCEA tuning. You can still play the song as written in standard tuning but the 4th string will sound an octave higher than it should be.

HUMORESKE

Czechoslovakia

Ukulele tuing: gCEA

Antonin Dvorak

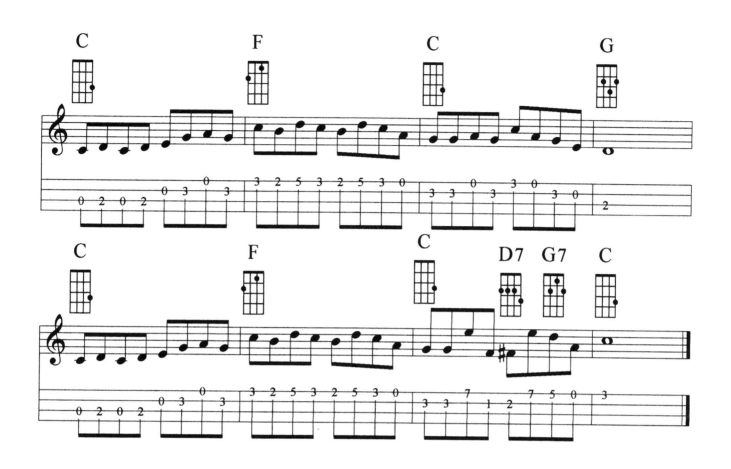

Czechoslovakia stamps

IL ETAIT UNE BERGERE

France

Ukulele tuning: gCEA

Traditional

KUJAWIAK

Poland

Ukulele tuning: gCEA

Traditional

JUANITA
Spain

Ukulele tuning: gCEA

Traditional

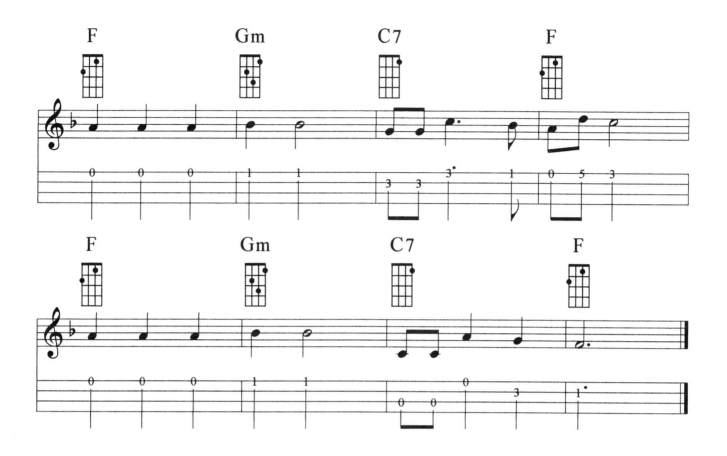

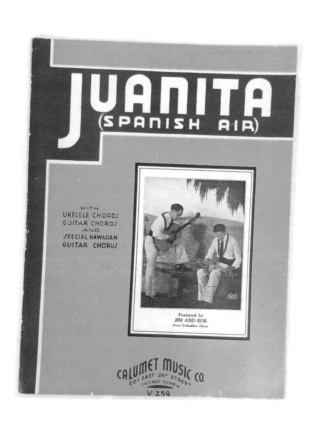

THE KERRY DANCE

Low G tuning: GCEA

Ireland

James L. Molloy

Because of the wide range of this song, the ukulele is tuned to Low G. This tuning.replaces the 4th string and tunes it a full octave lower than standard "g" in gCEA tuning. This enables the song to be put into a more playable key where the high notes are also lowered. You can still play the song in standard tuning, but the notes on the 4th string will sound an octave higher than they should. Listen to the online audio to hear the correct pitch.

NOTE: Several books are available from Centerstream Publications for Low G tuning.

LA CUCARACHA

Mexico

Ukulele tuning: gCEA

Traditional

LA PALOMA
Spain

Ukulele tuning: gCEA

Sebastian Yradier

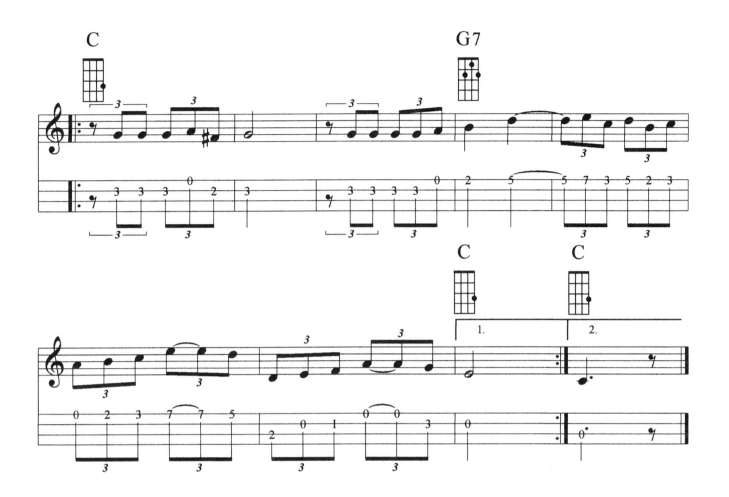

THE LITTLE DUSTMAN

Netherlands

Ukulele tuning: gCEA

Traditional

See how the lit - tle dust - man through win - dows thrusts his head, he

looks for sleep - y chil - dren who should be tucked in bed. And

as each wear - y head he spies, he___ throws dust in their eyes.

Go to sleep, close your eyes and dream your sleep a - way.___

MI CABALLO BLANCO

Chile

Ukulele tuning: gCEA

Traditional

LOCH LOMOND

Scotland

Ukulele tuning: gCEA

Traditional

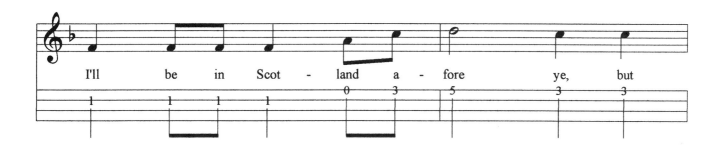

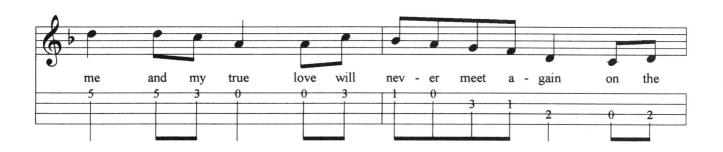

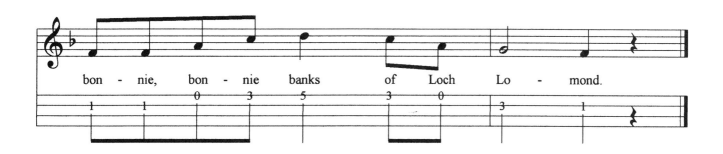

MARCHING TO PRETORIA

South Africa

Ukulele tuning: gCEA

Traditional

MARCHING TO PRAETORIA

The song was sung by British troops as they marched to the city of Pretoria, the principal battleground of the Boer War between England and the Dutch Afrikaners in South Africa.

MEXICAN HAT DANCE

Ukulele in Low G tuning: GCEA   Mexico   Traditional

The Hat →

MO LI HUA

China

Ukulele in Low G tuning: GCEA

Traditional

NORWEGIAN DANCE

Ukulele tuning: gCEA

Edvard Grieg

Norwegian composer Edvard Greig is especially known for his *Piano Concerto in A Minor* and *Peer Gynt Suite* which includes *In The Hall of the Mountain King, Morning Mood, Anitra's Dance* and *Åse's Death*.

O CANADA

Ukulele tuning: gCEA

Canada

Calixa Lavallee

"O Canada" is the National Anthem of Canada.

OH! SUSANNA

United States

Ukulele tuning: gCEA

Stephen Foster

I__ come from Al - a - bam - a with my ban - jo on my knee, I'm
I__ had a dream the oth - er night, when ev - 'ry thing was still, I__

goin' to Lou - si - an - a my__ true love for to see. It__
thought I saw Su - san - na a - com - in' down the hill. The

rained all night the day I left, the weath - er it was dry, the
buck wheat cake was in her mouth, the tear was in her eye, said

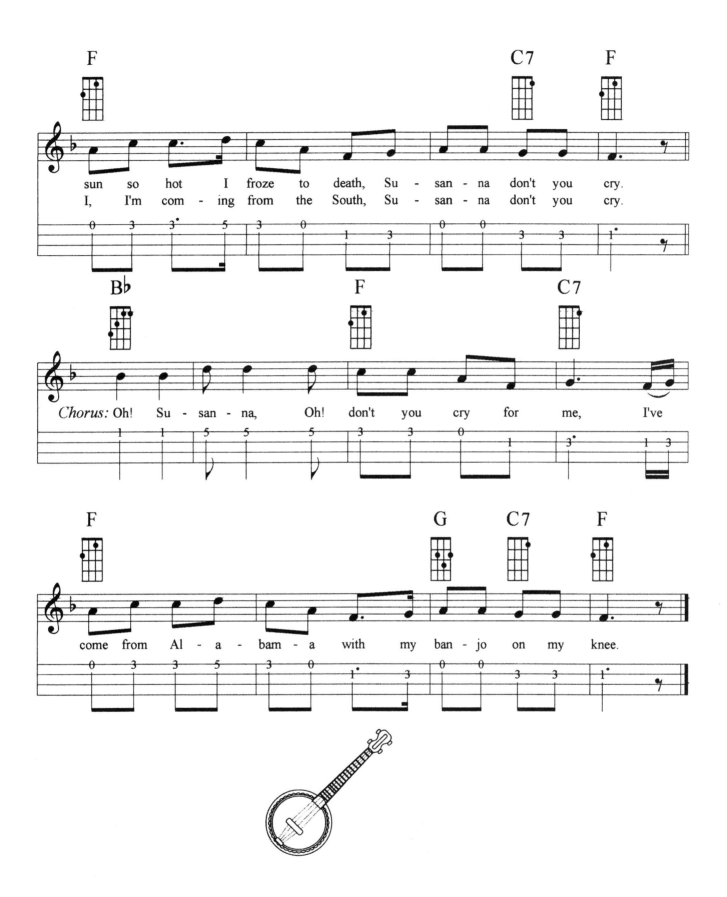

SAKURA

Japan

Ukulele tuning: gCEA

Traditional

SANTA LUCIA

Italy

Ukulele tuning: gCEA

Traditional

Now 'neath the sil - ver moon o - cean is glow - ing,
Here balm - y breez - es blow, pure joys in - vite__ us,

o'er the calm bil - low soft winds are blow - ing;
and as we gent - ly, row, all things de - light us.

Hark, how the sail - or's cry joy - ous - ly ech - oes nigh:

San - ta__ Lu__ ci - a! San - ta Lu - ci - a! San - ta Lu - ci - a.

SCARBORO FAIR

England   Traditional

Ukulele tuning: gCEA

SCOTLAND THE BRAVE

Scotland

Ukulele tuning: gCEA

Traditional

SILENT NIGHT

Ukulele tuning: gCEA

Austria

Franz Gruber

SOUTH AUSTRALIA
Australia

Ukulele tuning: gCEA

Traditional

In South Aus - tra - lia I was born, heave a - way, haul a - way, in

South Aus - tra - lia 'round Cape Horn, we're bound for South Aus - tra - lia.

Haul a - way, you roll - ing king, heave a - way, haul a - way,

haul a - way, Oh hear me sing, we're bound for South Aus - tra - lia.

STILL, STILL, STILL
Austria

Ukulele tuning: gCEA

Traditional

SUR LE PONT D'AVIGNON

France

Ukulele tuning: gCEA

Traditional

WALTZING MATILDA

Words by A.P. "Banjo" Paterson

Australia

Marie Cowan

TWO GUITARS
Russia

Ukulele tuning: gCEA

Traditional Gypsy

Fm   Cm   G7   Cm

♩=120

Fm   Cm   G7   Cm

Fm   Cm   G7   Cm

Fm   Cm   G7   Cm